TO WHITEY
& THE CRACKER JACK

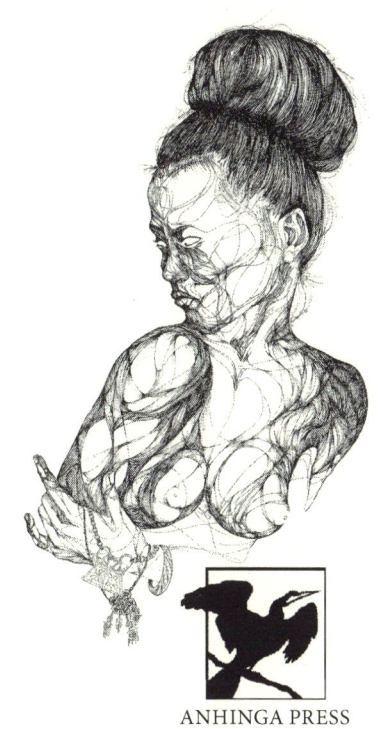

ANHINGA PRESS

TO WHITEY
& THE CRACKER JACK

POEMS
HAUNTIE

2016 ROBERT DANA-ANHINGA PRIZE
Selected by Evie Schockley

ANHINGA PRESS
TALLAHASSEE, FLORIDA 2017

Copyright © May Yang 2017
All rights reserved under
International and Pan-American Copyright Conventions.

No portion of this book may be reproduced in any form without the written permission of the publisher, except by a reviewer, who may quote brief passages in connection with a review for a magazine or newspaper.

Cover Image: May Yang
Design, production: Jay Snodgrass
Type Styles: body text in Arno Pro and titles in Futura PT

Library of Congress Cataloging-in-Publication Data
To Whitey & the Cracker Jack — First Edition
ISBN — 978-1-934695-53-1
Library of Congress Cataloging Card Number — 2017937005

Anhinga Press Inc. is a nonprofit corporation dedicated wholly to the publication and appreciation of fine poetry and other literary genres.

For personal orders, catalogs, and information, write to:

ANHINGA PRESS
P.O. Box 3665 • Tallahassee, Florida 32315
Website: www.anhingapress.org • Email: info@anhingapress.org

Published in the United States by Anhinga Press
Tallahassee, Florida • First Edition, 2017

THE ROBERT DANA-ANHINGA PRIZE WINNERS

2016 Hauntie *To Whitey & the Cracker Jack*
2015 Elizabeth A.I. Powell *Willy Loman's Reckless Daughter
    or Living Truthfully Under Imaginary Circumstances*
2014 Robin Beth Schaer *Shipbreaking*
2013 Bethany Schultz Hurst *Miss Lost Nation*
2012 Anna Ross *If a Storm*
2011 Rosalynde Vas Dias *Only Blue Body*
2010 Kimberly Burwick *Horses in the Cathedral*
2009 Gretchen Steele Pratt *One Island*
2008 Rhett Iseman Trull *The Real Warnings*
2007 Kenneth Hart *Uh Oh Time*
2006 Meredith Walters *All you have to do is ask*
2005 Sandy Longhorn *Blood Almanac*
2004 Joshua Poteat *Ornithologies*
2003 Deborah Landau *Orchidelirium*
2002 Erika Meitner *Inventory at the All-night Drugstore*
2001 Patti White *Tackle Box*
2000 Ruth L. Schwartz *Singular Bodies*
1999 Kathleen Wakefield *Notations on the Visible World*
1998 Julia B. Levine *Practicing for Heaven*
1997 Michele Wolf *Conversations During Sleep*
1996 Keith Ratzlaff *Man Under a Pear Tree*
1995 Ann Neelon *Easter Vigil*
1994 Frank X. Gaspar *Mass for the Grace of a Happy Death*
1993 Janet Holmes *The Physicist at the Mall*
1992 Earl S. Braggs *Hat Dancer Blue*
1991 Jean Monahan *Hands*
1989 Nick Bozanic *The Long Drive Home*
1988 Julianne Seeman *Enough Light to See*
1987 Will Wells *Conversing with the Light*
1986 Robert Levy *The Whistle Maker*
1985 Judith Kitchen *Perennials*
1984 Sherry Rind *The Hawk in the Backyard*
1983 Ricardo Pau-Llosa *Sorting Metaphors*

Preface

I write this in remembrance of the countless times the United Nations would not acknowledge that the Soviet Union was supplying chemical-biological warfare agents to the Pathet Lao to be used on our people. I write this to mark the many moments Hmong have attempted to represent their suffering among white politicians, who told them that they did not suffer in the face of danger. I write this because I have to mourn loss, conjure the past, and move to heal. For my grandmother who was a slave under French and Hmong officials, for my father who was enslaved as a prisoner of war in Pathet Lao concentration camps, and for Hmong orphans without a totem to speak for them. I am HAUNTIE, the auntie-mother you have cast into the margins of your lives. Demonized for loving among men, for rearing children without a father, and for healing the sick with quick magic.

CONTENTS

PART I
RETRIBUTION

Vengeance is a Gift	3
A Simple Trajectory	4
The Sub Altern Ate Capital Reality	5
Mind Power	6
In Our Fire	7
Head Money Pt. II	8
Make Me Human or Give Me Death	10
Dear Foreign Entity,	12
Zen Keeper	13

PART II
HAUNTINGS

Knowing Grandma is Knowing Self	17
Thirsty Thirsty Mekong	18
Unlike Myself	19
Life is Beyond You	20
This Sadness	21
Gestures of Time	22
A Meter for Time	23
Cycles	24

PART III
MONSTERS IN THEIR MOUTHS

Madness is a Tool	27
To Play Your Image like a Fool	30
we needed to accuse.	31
alive	32
Law of the Father	33
Two & Two	34
Shadow & Act	35

PART IV
HOME

Mourning Lesson	39
First Generation, Displaced	40
My Skin is From	41
Niam Qub	42
Mapping Home	43
Vertical Dreams	44
Meeting Place	45
Mother's Tempo	46
Pressing	47
Another Tomorrow	48

PART V

ALL OUR WORTH

A Frequent Tension	51
A Heart Speaks	52
of being bastard	53
notes on how to move	54
You Wish Your Life Weren't So	55
Head Money Pt. 1	56
Disorder	57
For the First Time	58
To All My Friends	60
Nothing is	61
Hymn of Your Ancestors	63

PART VI

AFTERTHOUGHTS

non-eurocentric Art	67
conceptual Art	68
bastard-ry will set you free	69
The Yin & Yang Complex	70
Noj Wifi	71
Standing next to whiteness	72
uninscribed & liberated	73
Seeking	74
Resolution	75
Archive	76
The Imagined Past	77
Origins	78
Being Whole	79
Face Book	80
deep know-nothings	81
Ancient Japanese Poem	82
Creativity	83

**TO WHITEY
& THE CRACKER JACK**

for all the times you've heard our pain without feeling

PART I
RETRIBUTION

The beat of a jungle warfare runs through my veins, and i am here to drink the blood of a millennium of men dressed in stars and stripes, from purple mountains majesty across the fruited plains of a native mother's womb.

Vengeance is a Gift

A Simple Trajectory

Some time ago pale bodies slipped into Indochina and harvested slave bodies to sow opium and mine silver. These slaves developed a dependency on this unsustainable and temporary economy, becoming heavily addicted to this intoxicating flower. Some no longer planted their own food or raised their own livestock. A body from this time was that of my my grandmother's. Impoverished – she was – mind, body and soul. Strung out on the tar of this little flower, forgetting how and when to love her children. A body that came to life through hers was my father's. And so it was that this boy would walk miles to school with maybe, sometimes hardly ever, a palm-full of rice and a single chili pepper to sustain his body for the duration of the day.
    Night would fall,
   and day would rise.
Then a secret war crept up so loud white minds shut it out
and all of humanity hushed it from the West to its East
and my grandfather went to war on the side that would win
doing these things, they couldn't believe in
and maybe it was that they won, maybe
but the shackles of this flower brought my mother to my father
and the shackles of this flower brought my body to America

          "Here I am," i'll say.
         Here I am and I have to stay.

What are you? Where are you from? What did you come from?

              i am a potent flower
         stringing out your mind on line after line
      from the womb of a history birthed from white memory
                i am American
               i am good at forgetting

The Sub Altern Ate Capital Reality

For some time now i have had the pleasurable power to be of my self,
                               apart from global capitalism

                 i have held onto my own complexion,

but they will eventually drink this self to bone,
because i have never been
                               re presented

within their dinner table talk.

Burning chimneys and the tinkering of glass from the shadows of servants,
chitting-chatting definitions that do not define the souls of the inside,

                 for they have always lacked that matter,

but define the contours of the outside through false negations.

One day i'll have their skin for dinner
red wine please,

                                         rare.

Mind Power

i could bend spoons,
so that every time America decides to open its fat mouth
and devour bodies whole on silver,
real life duende.

Did you think our blood was for dinner tonight?
You just got duped.

You live in privilege
within the pages of history
Your skin and bone
blood and spit
are spoken of – remembered.

i am the dust on your ground
that you trample on.
i am the tree in the jungle
that you cut down
to write on.

All that ink on the pages of my skin,
dust to dust
and ash to ash.

When the rain falls we'll seep into the dirt
resurrect as mountains and valleys
to cut your body in half
divide you by the sea and the hillside
and your spit and blood and bone and skin will feed us
once again

In Our Fire

Head Money Pt. II

You used to wear a lock across your chest
hung from one tit to the other
Your slave masters never let you forget
who you were

They cut your tongue
left you with a cloud of quiet pillows
to murmur to

        "A spirit lock to bind you," they said.

A lover twice removed lined the back of your neck
with pink and green patterns
treacherous markings reminding you
of your place

Never letting you forget that you are without tongue
Koj lub dab tsho os
they were afraid of you

        "Let us keep our heads," they said.

Pog los niam tais stitched it below your neck
every single new year
your dress shirt and suit is no good without one
you will look naked

With nothing to speak for you
when back is turned
to desiring slave masters
        "You are incomplete" they'll say.

    for a slave master measures worth through the markings of a tag

A teacher now anchors a map in the middle of your back – a letter with a pin
caught in your flesh like a hook
reminding you to learn their sounds

"Speak them in your sleep" they say.

Aye
Mbhe
Sí
Dee
Eeh
Eff – uh

You know these murmurs are not yours,
but they will do.

Fitted with a new tongue you smile
each corner of your mouth a spear
a red rope whips back and forth between plump cheeks
when you laugh it slaps the ground before your feet

Eyeh
Emh
Nht
Ursh!

For all the times I've been without tongue
listening to the cries of slave master children
giving them medicine from my finger tips
holding their pain in my liver, lung and head

to be mine – this tongue – to be mine.

Silent for centuries
slave no more
I am my own sounds
and so you shall listen

Make Me Human or Give Me Death

This matters because i've lived on that side of life that you all have made for me

partitioned
the orphaned one

i who carry the fire from your ashes, the chains of your people,
and the residual sting from an incessant yellow rain

This matters because i realize something you thought i would never even know!

that i have a mouth
and a throat!
my body remembers
the flesh, this flesh, my flesh is woke.

This matters because my mouth will let me be myth, no more!

i carry this fire and i carry it well and you will feel this heat
when you come up next to me
i will press you with this light until your sweat turns to boiling hot water
to relieve me
i will lick you, whip you with these flames until your body breaks
like mine to free me

and you will crawl and unlearn love and joy like i did
and you will cry and call for your God like I did.

because i am myth, no more!

Feel me.

and this flame which burned my grandfather's house down
and this light which shackled my grandmother's body down
and this heat which scorched my father's spirit down
will look onto you and take you like it took me too

its
white
light

Because it matters
and this is how you will know me
Because i matter
and this is how you will fear me
Because i can be silent, no more!

to this white lie

or give me death.

4/26/2016

Dear Foreign Entity,

You will never be able to separate me,
my whole self,
from my body.

Only death is imparted that power.

Signed,
The Self

Zen Keeper

A house
Bamboo floors no shoes
Wind like spring pressing window
Soft and pale

white man honk horn at me
white boy middle finger in air at me
white dad put tongue on lip say, "Fuck me."

I am your house of Zen
Quiet eastern eyes
Place of Pleasure

A house
Hmong knives fresh blood
Hot kettle bitter steeped tea
Shrill and scream

One strike you lose one leg
Two strike you lose two leg
Three strike you lose third leg

I tell you be calm
Let it go
Place of Peace

PART II
HAUNTINGS

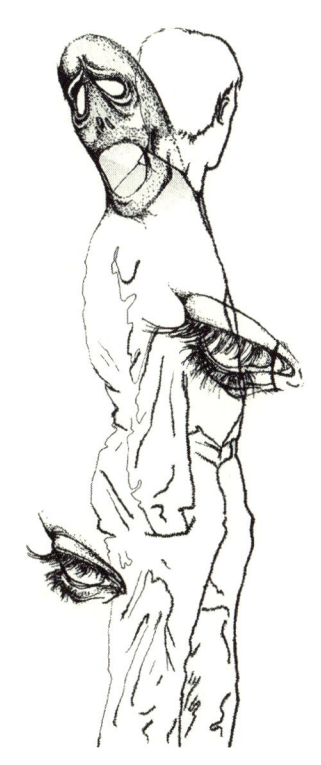

Knowing Grandma is Knowing Self

"To live this long you must want death as much as I do. To be an orphan and to watch life pass you by, even the one you loved the longest. Do you know misery? You should. It makes you a better person. In life, everyone will want, and it is this longing that makes us suffer" – Grandma
August 17, 2013 9:30 a.m.

A lesson on self-care and self-love in a post modern world from a pre modern woman.

in the now

Thirsty Thirsty Mekong

A million little Hmong babies on the river's shore
swept under green foam within these greying waves
there's my sister, and my brother
a cousin twice removed
their bodies slowly churned into this world's core

I saw a dragon swallow them away
he took them with the storm
with the lightening and the rain
to a cave beneath our feet
another place for them to stay

In the bellies of the tourists are a million little Hmong babies
catfish curry at the Mekong Breeze
they wonder how this fish
got to be so big, so sweet.

Do you remember what mother said to me?
Red hands smearing gold beneath the waist of our aunties
to see if the bees would come back to retrieve their precious honey

A million little Hmong babies that never touched the light of day
I saw them sleep but never wake
nestled under brilliant amber
caught in the eyes of a stinging Red bee.

Unlike Myself

i do not look Asian
i do not look like a Woman
i do not look like I am from any Place
i do not look very interesting at all.

i look like my uncle
when he was a small child

the one who used to put his face up to the pigs and mimic them,

                    Kwoigh! Kwoigh! Kwoigh!

the brother my mother loved the most
with the high forehead and the bubbling laughter

the one lost as a sacrifice for the silence of many
Was it with a cloth soaked in opium?

buried beneath a mound of moist jungle dirt
Was he still breathing?

That is who i look like.

The one my grandmother saw first, when she actually saw

                                                  me.

Life is Beyond You

because they placed it in a jar and dropped it in a river,
and your flesh is left on the side,
below the heavy banana tree,
whose fruit you could never pick,
of which your eyes will stare at for eternity,
because your mother and your father have no legs,
and your sister and brother made it to the other side,
and no one is there to close your eyes.

So you stare at the yellow fruit,
and they will turn brown with decay
and so will the two bright lights from the middle of your head.

To the one I look the most like

This Sadness

with the weight of my kin
it sags
and each vessel
that it has hung upon
stretches with time.

and time is long
it is forever
and wraps back into itself.

a ripping of the cells
and the movement of my mind
sends flesh
a part from flesh
and i am sad.

no victims here
just floatin'

on the Mekong.
Laos 1975

Same struggle,
different breath

She hands the pot to me,
tells me to fill it with water

Thick mouths white grey bristles
smack on Marlboros in wait

Smoke roils along grunts
between bare-footed children

Gold bells curdle blood back
and forth from stove to foul plate

A quick spit to salt the food
cleanse earth of forgotten totems

Same struggle,
different breath

Gestures of Time

Pain is the residue of something – past
Pain is the sound of what is felt – present
Pain is the substance from without – absence
Pain is the negative space that carves – future.

A Meter for Time

Cycles

The future is a shadow
it awaits us
beckons us
compels us
lets us dream.

It hails us
calls upon us by our name

but it has no voice
it only has our needs

the future is never complete
a long and narrow absence

Being next to death,
i know the future can never be.

Life,
A circle always folding back into itself
compressed.

        We are familiar with shadows
   A flat collapse of absence and presence
         We are each other's ghosts

to be unheard of is,

to be without –

                          no time given

to the thought of me –

                          no second to my word

                          no movement to my steps

still,

i am every revolution that turns in you
a winding clock
which expounds your cohesion
like every new day
when i finally arrive upon you

                          i am reincarnate

always something new
in every death
you have gifted me

i've died in the many lives you have marked as free

and still,
        reincarnate

                          of genocide outside your time

PART III
MONSTERS IN THEIR MOUTHS

Madness is a Tool

It hails us across street corners,
from park benches,
from rumbling throats under triangle tarps,
from beneath arcs of concrete,

between alleyways and bus stops,
between plaster and prescription pills,
between normality and genius.

It reminds us of a constant uncertainty,
that our totems are not absolute,
that this pain must come from somewhere,
that their sounds are our own ghosts,

which refuse to hide,
which seek refuge on our minds,
which speak only to be healed.

and

It never forgets that we are its audience.

To Play Your Image like a Fool

Whether it scares you
                                        or secures you

In your suburban leather couches,
or coffee houses.

Whether it intrigues you
                                        or reflects you

In your Cadillac-chevy-benzos,
or restaurant bistros.

Me,
Hauntie

The one with tiger claws and china eyes

Me,
Hauntie

The one with ninja stars and chopstick flies

Me,
Hauntie

The one with your god but I aint eat no dog!

Me,
Hauntie

The aunty-mother of your lost children and a demon among men as children,

we would throw our toys into the middle of the room
cover our eyes with a blanket
count to twenty
lift the covers

we would charge the President Teddy bear
and Miss America Barbie of being evil
of being monsters
who moved when we weren't looking.

        we knew that they wanted to kill us.

we needed to accuse

trauma is a suspended action –

Bigger Brother would carry knives in the dark when we slept
he would stab our toys in the night
for simply being

alive

Law of the Father

it is everywhere
in kitchen pots and silver spoons
under blankets and children's books
in love ballads and modern tunes

it is within you
in the gap between your hinges
under covers, cries and cringes
in late nights and liquor binges

it is without you
in rooms whose doors you've closed
under brooms in filth you've thrown
in the casket of a master you've known

                                          take him down when he faces you
                                             when his gaze is fixed upon you
                                     when you know you are no longer of two
                           but one, just you, and free, through and through

Two & Two

Two and two are three
They are busy as bees can be
When the bee stings the coochi
And the coochi is free
Two and two are three!

Two and two are three
When mama told me I was four
Don't look out the door
When the Reds kill the poor
Two and two are four!

Two and two are four
Now the Reds got my aunty on the floor
So you better run and hide
Keep your tears in your eyes
Two and two no more!

Two and two no more
Cause my dad his feet real sore
He be runnin' he be hidin'
In the jungles Reds be lying
Two and two no more!

Shadow & Act

the moment the one who hails sees the flesh and matter
and substance and form and figure of their rendering

a quiver in their pale knees

& Scene

PART IV

HOME

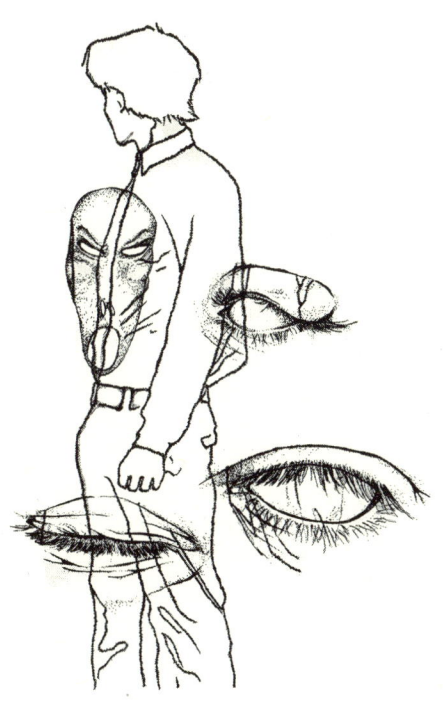

There are eight kids in my family.
I am the third youngest.
We used to play a game called House.
There was always a store keeper, a teacher and a masseuse.
We liked materials, money and relaxing.
We used to chase our 6 wild rabbits in the backyard.
That was when I learned that rabbits could scream.
One summer my cousin convinced me to wash peaches in the plastic pool.
We got itchy after swimming in it.
During the winter we used to squirt the hose into the pit behind the chimney in the backyard.
Frogs would come out and we would put them in the plastic pool.
One morning I was passing a frog to my sister and it jumped off my hand.
She stepped on it.
When she lifted up her foot it started to hop away with its pretty translucent pink and blue stomach trailing out from its back end.
"Quick! We have to take it out of its misery!" she yelled, or maybe I yelled.
So she grabbed my mother's black platform heel, it was the 90s, and she smacked it with one hard whack.

WHAP!

We walked into our house and stared out from the window of our porch into the grey clouds, and hoped that it would not haunt our dreams that night.

Mourning Lesson

Fresno, CA

First Generation, Displaced

"I know my robe is going to fit me well. I tried it on at the gates of hell,"
                                                                                              she thought

as she passed through her mother's garden and into the unsightly world
she would soon know.

With a deep sigh, and a full first breath
all the sweetness and freshness of fruit and soft ground would fall back
into it's void.

A nothingness,

                                                                                                        forgotten

with the new line of capital time.

                                                      i was there, and then never more.

                                                                     March 8, 1991

My Skin is From

The ghetto
The valley
The jungles
The war camp
Yellow rain
The reds
The river
The city
The village
The internet

i could go on,
but you could not piece it together

In my dreams she was a silhouette in the kitchen

                                            her back to me

pressed against the sink with the sound of clinking dishes

                                          no voice

and two gold hoops swinging from jaw.

                                                          Niam Qub

Mapping Home

Body

A meeting place between the many times that came before it
These times, the trajectories that brought me to be here now

Body

A passing form
like a flower
the slowest moment of rupture in a single time

in time – body as memory
through time – body as home
with time – body as matter

i am body, yet i do not claim body
i never meant to sever with ink

What is the act of mark making, if not to define?
And what is definition, if not without exclusion?
What is exclusion, if not the cutting of matter?

The abstraction of cartography occurs
when the difference of parts is blurred
and lines are no longer visible
and place is not but visceral.

That time in the prepubescent stage of my life when we were so poor i had to wear a pair of pants that didn't have a button twice a week without a training bra or deodorant

and we foraged the expired canned foods that were donated to us from the community, which sat in a large pile on our porch.

We was that fam on the block, yo

and my sister and i wondered how the hell to make canned pumpkin taste like the pumpkin pie from the store on a cold winter day.

i keep telling myself that I'm never gonna be there again in any of my life forms.

Vertical Dreams

i am straddling memory and the present tension
muscles turning into stone from the weight of time
how do you understand me in all of your knowing?

i am standing at crossroads
and there are many of them, one on top of the other
and they are not flat
and i could not just lie on the ground to rest and breathe

but i would like to

to survive i must stand and hold them all together
with my feet pinned down like a needle binding seems
so that when people cross me
when they cut these paths
we can speak
and we can be together
for a moment in time

this is how i feel about myself.

Meeting Place

all of life was stripped, but i learned to put it back,
                                                eventually

jumbled it is, but i will smooth it out,
                                    eventually

Mother's Tempo

Pressing

summertime sadness
summertime blues
summertime worries
summertime noons

a heat presses on sun licked skin
with each sweat a tear
and every pant

a sigh
a grief
a broken wish

these nights return like the warm mouth of my mother
calling upon my name to exercise my right to life
a steaming chorus for a laborious chore

6/20/2016

pain becomes

the pouring of the coffee into mug
the stir of a spoon in cold soup
a clink of the comb on porcelain
some wind sounding out aches along these branches

i forget my keys forget my phone and where i parked

i forget to eat the soup and drink my tea to read the news and water old roots

i forget my everyday

       in place of some thing that pushes against my present tense
            rubbing chaffing folding against me
a thing I know too well and too soon to forget it for today to remember today for tomorrow it leaves me no breath to remember where i placed my keys to the trunk of this house.

Another Tomorrow

PART V

ALL OUR WORTH

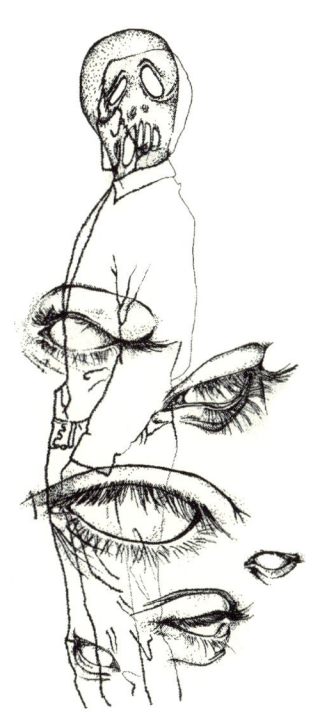

the Hmong experience is many
we are a whole body

when a single nerve moves,
is severed
strained
or in pain

we feel it all
all of us
we feel it all

                    the transference of memory,
                        i feel the loss

i feel the blood soaked deep in soil nourishing sweet plantains for the animals
        the flesh picked at by catfish, later arriving in hot soups

maybe i am alone in this
like calm mornings when you are the only one awake
and all the rest of the nearest world are asleep

                    pain moves me to write.

A Frequent Tension

my problem is that i am not so advanced in the language of reason,
and that is why i am an illegitimate child.
no one will feed me the fruits

of my labor
of my labor
of my labor

to cultivate this flesh is a mastering of the tongue first

the taste of reason
the buds of truth

and only then
can my heart feel a beating

thump
thump
thump

life is something to be spoken
have i life, or am i spoken?

A Heart Speaks

It is harder for us –

orphans

to overcome the greatest struggle of all,
which is to act on what we believe in –
our own truth.

If all the world is a stage
they really took out my story line,
but in the end,
i am my own mise-en-scéne.

Even if i am unremembered,
and dismembered
from some family of society
i am my own.

of being bastard

a strange life it is then
when your people walk the earth with such stealth
that there is no residue of their place

                          taking form

and when the captors hail us to speak
they are caught among our steps
like geese amidst a wildfire

                          in our conjuring

we leave a silence so penetrative
you shake in its absence
displaced sounds echo

                          back and forth

        reverberating your memories like broken window frames
        chattering as teeth in the mouths of wind spirits

                                              notes on how to move

You Wish Your Life Weren't So

Fucking political,

That you could be one of those nonsensical artists who play with light and time and space and think that it's the shit just to frame that – shit.

That you could be one of those nonsensical lame-o scholars of war who play with neurons and electrons and atoms and ions and think that it's just the shit just to blow that – shit.

That you could be one of those nonsensical historians of humanity's past who play with dates and fabricate ed. facts and power and erasures and think that it's the shit just to write that – shit.

That you could be one of those nonsensical politicians who talk and walk and sleep and eat and confess their sins to the blind on pillars and think that it's the shit just to pretend that – shit.

but you are not one of these

You are only
the *other*

Head Money Pt. 1

Daddy said i was worth a single bee
i sat on the ground
wondering what it meant to be worth something
he laughed

Daddy said i was worth a dollar –
maybe, and he sat there
wondering what it meant to be worth something
i laughed

Some New Years, i put on my spirit lock
and wear pink and green sashes that bind
these breasts and this flesh
wondering what it means to be worth something

Disorder

i know it well like my backbone
a groovy dissonance
situated on these wide hips
i carry the tears of my ancestors
ready to breath new life
and i hold it all in
every breath an ancient step
every blink a river of blood
this loneliness is mine
an echo of the wind
which sits on your shoulder
holding every word

they pound out this life in familiar intonations

so that i could be this human at this time
along that side of pain on this side of life
pinned to these bones always sounding

they pound out this life in familiar intonations

For the First Time

i know nothing of writing
it knows nothing of me

                      an unsettling stranger

yet i long for it
as it longs for me

                      an unnerving meeting

it stares at me, empty
i stare back, cautious

                      an unwavering touch

        she grasps at the pencil with ungainly hands, veins like rope,
                    skin like plaster

                      i ask her,
                      No
                      i tell her,

show me

                your house in the refugee camp
                the one you miss and think of

draw me

                        its shapes with the candy counter
                        the one you laughed and ate at

write me

                        how you knew of love there with grandpa
                        the one you were without children with

she takes the instrument
presses down four sides of a wall
lined across whiteness

"there," she utters
for the first time, she makes her mark.

That I could be this human at this time
breathing, looking, seeing, smelling

That I could be this moment at this time
resting, calmly moving, feeling

That I could be this excellence at this time
sudden, changed, peaceful, & woke

To all my friends who have been with me in weakness
when water falls rush down my two sides

To all my friends who have felt me in anguish
when this earthen back breaks between the crack of two blades

To all my friends who have held me in rage
when fire tears through swallows behind tight grins

I know you
I see you
I hear you

Although the world is silent around you

I know you
I see you
I hear you

To All My Friends

Nothing is

nothing is greater than you
you are life
your body dirt
your blood water
your soul wind
your hair leaves
your teeth stone
your heart fire
your flesh breath
you are life
nothing is greater than you

Don't be afraid to leave
We support your life
When you think ill
There is medicine for every ailment

Don't be afraid to leave
When they beckon you to come back
To drink our water and feel our sound
It is only to heal

Don't be afraid to leave
When some are cruel and eyes are sharp
It is because they are hurting
And desiring of your light

Don't be afraid to leave
There is no absence in your footsteps
You are afraid to forget us
But more afraid we will neglect you

Don't be afraid to leave
We would never forget you
You are always remembered
Your body fully embraced

Don't be afraid to leave
We have always packed you chicken
And fresh rice in banana leaves
Water, even chili, because we love you

Don't be afraid to leave
If you perish we will call upon you
And fit you with a cow or six
Guide you back home in our song

Don't be afraid to leave
Your heart is never apart
In your dreams you will feel us
We should never forget you

Hymn of Your Ancestors

PART VI
AFTERTHOUGHTS

non-eurocentric Art

losing function
since capital came over for dinner
and stayed forever

conceptual Art

takes form for granted
dislocates the context
appropriates the flesh

Ideology killed relatives time never allowed me to have.

1950 - present

i am such
a bastard-ous child
it's only prophetic

bastard-ry will set you free

There will always be problems to solutions.
Cats are to dogs as sky is to diesel.

The Yin & Yang Complex

measurement is merely a definition of some potential energy
the act of consuming
embodying that energy, that frequency,
which is also matter
allows for being
for living

the internet is real
not because we say it is
but because we live it

Noj Wifi

Standing next to whiteness

i feel that we are,
competing bodies of knowledge.

This is the stench of nothing.
Strange – because it is unidentifiable
to you
Unidentifiable – because you have always known
something

never
no thing

You will not make reason here
You will not know me or of me
You will leave, and take no reason from here

This
is mine.

Look into
the vastness of nothing,
and think

that could be you.

uninscribed & liberated

The Sky is Never the Same
i look to the stars for the ends of time.

Seeking

Resolution

                                        death comes in many ways,
                                        but forever has one ending.

i will turn you into a fiction
and maybe you will have more potency then

Archive

The Imagined Past

in the dark i cast no shadow
what is left is only a body of wonder
with no body to ponder

Residue
c. All Our Life

the best part of life is that we are human
and we are not rooted anywhere

really.

Origins

The masculine does not read me. My lyrical potency has got enough venom to severe the flesh between their stilts.

let
them
fall

Being Whole

in times like these,
you have nothing to claim,
but your own image.

Face Book

Humans – animals who think humor is the act of pretending to throw the ball for a dog, when all the dog sees is a deceitful being. How human are we?

deep know-nothings

The post modernized person displaces their energy in and through objects to process it when other beings are not present or desirably present.

Television, internet, pencil, car, paper, video game, garden, art, nano technology, microphone, refrigerator.

These objects serve a specific purpose of making people feel separate from the real.

We watch the news to produce an order that differentiates us from non-human beings so that life may feel less vulnerable. We are fixated on potential energy, possibility and the near future. What could go great, could also be a catastrophe. We must know truths, facts and finite outcomes so that death may feel more further away.

The past is always a regression, and understanding it is knowing that we have excelled.

Do you like my poem?
        Seeing is believing. Knowledge is power.

                              Our Karma is in our thumbs.

Ancient Japanese Poem

Creativity

Postmodernity's umbrella term for human preoccupation with actions that consciously separate us from the subconscious awareness of decay, death and dying. Thoughts which are always there, but never spoken. Art is the possibility of life, and can never be real absence – another sight of death.

Being creative is a healthy action, no human being can not live without ever having created anything!

The system compels you to, even if you are performing cheap labor in a sweatshop in Los Angeles, you have produced an object to rectify another's life, if not only your own.

Empowerment is not as real as it seems. It is something to get us by here in America. Like my cousin said, 100 U.S. dollars can buy 5 people in Thailand to perform a month's worth of labor in a Toyota factory. Which it did.

I drive a Toyota.
He made it.

A Neocapitalist Love Ballad
c. 2000 B.L. "before liberation"

About the Author

HAUNTIE is a persona derived from the experiences of May Yang, a first-generation Hmong American woman. Her writing is shaped from life within the Hmong diaspora, the teachings of her grandmothers, aunts, and single-mother *Maumtsov*. She is influenced by the work, art and magic of Frantz Fanon, June Jordan, Octavia E. Butler, Adrian Piper, Ana Mendieta, Carrie Mae Weems, Lil' Buck and David Blaine. She believes in using the power of language to simultaneously explore and test our freedoms as human beings.